NETWORK MARKETING - 'SLOW START TO SUPER SUCCESS'

TIPS & STRATEGIES TO ATTAIN SUCCESS BY MR. BHUPENDRA PAL

SUPREET BATRA

Xpress Publishing
An imprint of Notion Press

No.8, 3rd Cross Street,CIT Colony,
Mylapore, Chennai, Tamil Nadu-600004

Copyright © Supreet Batra
All Rights Reserved.

ISBN 978-1-63633-213-0

This book has been published with all efforts taken to make the material error-free after the consent of the author. However, the author and the publisher do not assume and hereby disclaim any liability to any party for any loss, damage, or disruption caused by errors or omissions, whether such errors or omissions result from negligence, accident, or any other cause.

While every effort has been made to avoid any mistake or omission, this publication is being sold on the condition and understanding that neither the author nor the publishers or printers would be liable in any manner to any person by reason of any mistake or omission in this publication or for any action taken or omitted to be taken or advice rendered or accepted on the basis of this work. For any defect in printing or binding the publishers will be liable only to replace the defective copy by another copy of this work then available.

This book is dedicated to Mr. Bhupendra Pal, a top achiever in Network Marketing, whose constant support and success principles proved to be very supportive to write the book. He is a great guy, an embodiment of all the traits that can effectively build one's business.

Contents

Preface vii

Acknowledgements ix

1. Introduction & Background Mr. Bhupendra Pal — 1
2. Network Marketing For The First Time — 4
3. Rejections To A Source Of Motivation — 9
4. What 'next'? — 14
5. Opting Network Marketing As A Full-time Business — 21
6. Why Network Marketing? — 25
7. Why Should Women Do Network Marketing? — 38
8. Why Do Students Need "network Marketing"? — 42
9. What Are The Common Mistakes? How To Avoid And Correct Them? — 46
10. Importance Of Strong Character In Network Marketing — 55
11. Essential Skills To Become Successful In Network Marketing — 60
12. Invitation Skills — 66
13. Objection Handling Skills — 75
14. Presentation Skills — 81
15. Follow-up Skills — 89
16. Attributes Of A Successful Networker — 100
17. Conclusion — 116

About The Author — 119

Preface

Mr. Bhupendra Pal is a real example of dedication and hard work. He worked not only to survive and feed his family as maximum people do, but also to achieve a significant benchmark in his life.

He first understood the power of network marketing, and then gave his 100% to the business.

Breakthroughs came in his journey, but he never got affected because of the strong "Why" in him.

His attitude is to work with full interest and dedication, which made him tackle all the problems and difficulties with a smile—starting from 2008- to date. In the coming pages, we will know about the family background of Mr. Bhupendra Pal and his life journey till now.

Journey from a 'Wrist-watch to BMW.'

I am thankful to Sir that He gave his valuable time and helped me to complete this book. This book will motivate those who want to achieve something in life and create a benchmark.

This book will tell how anyone who follows a few success principles can become a seven-figure earner in network marketing. Anyone from any background can become a Network Marketing Superstar, who reads this book and works on it wholeheartedly.

High Income, **Right values & skills, Popularity, and Great Personality**

Above are the few outcomes that one can develop after reading, and implementing the points, shared in this book. The coming pages shall be a life-transforming experience for all.

Acknowledgements

I am overwhelmed with all humbleness and gratefulness to acknowledge my depth to all those who helped me to put these ideas and tips into something concrete.

I would like to express my special thanks of gratitude to 'Mr. Bhupendra Pal', despite his big busy schedules, guided me and gave me different ideas, tips, and values in making this book, unique. Mr. Bhupendra Pal gave me the golden opportunity to write this wonderful book 'Slow start to Super success' which is helpful in providing guidelines to advance one's level of skills in network marketing. Any attempt at any level can't be satisfactorily completed without the support and guidance of my parents and friend.

ONE
Introduction & Background Mr. Bhupendra Pal

"If you want to give light to others, you have to glow yourself."

Mr. Bhupendra Pal belongs to a humble, middle-class family from a small district, Fatehpur, Uttar Pradesh. The primary schooling till the 8th class was from a small village, after that he moved to district school for higher education.

He was outstanding in studies, as we all know; it in maximum families that if their sons or daughters are good in studies, they want them to get into a government job. The same was with him. His parents wanted him to prepare for UPSE and crack IAS exams. They wanted to see him as an IAS officer since childhood.

They kept conditioning his mind. So, he used to hear all sorts of examples motivating to become a government officer. But getting into a government job was not the stream of interest of Mr. Bhupendra Pal.

He wanted to become a successful person in life, but how to become successful was not clear. His relatives used to ask him –

"What do you want to do?"

"What do you want to become in life?"

He used to reply,

"I want to become a rich & successful person."

But the path becoming wealthy & successful was unknown. He knew that the only way to become successful was to join IIT and become an engineer. So, he started to move on the path suggested by people and got admission in IET Lucknow for engineering.

ppp

TWO
Network Marketing For the First time

"Life-changing opportunity of my life was Introduction to Network Marketing."

In college days, Mr. Bhupendra got an opportunity of network marketing from some of his seniors. Before this, network marketing was a new business to him.

It came in front of him when one of his seniors asked him,

"Are you ambitious?"

He replied, **"Yes, I am."**

Then seniors asked him to come to their hostel.

Mr. Bhupendra Pal went there and attended the Network Marketing plan presentation for the first time.

He couldn't understand anything of it. The only thing he could make out was that some educational products have to be bought and promoted, and then he will get some money.

Even without understanding entirely about the business, he still opted for it, all because he got impressed by the personality, speaking skills of seniors. He thought that it is an excellent chance to learn and to transform him. And, friendship with seniors will undoubtedly increase his reputation in College. Thus, he got a reason and joined them in this business.

There were no 'big reasons' for joining network marketing. In the beginning, he was so casual for the first three-four months that he couldn't do much in network marketing, but the seniors kept on pushing him, inviting him for the meetings, and guiding him. They felt that Mr. Bhupendra can do it and can achieve **'something big.'**

One fine day, one of the seniors forced him to join the meeting.

This meeting proved to be a turning point in his life as he saw many youngsters of his age earning a lot; they had great personality and communication skills also. There he saw many youths from IIT Delhi and other prominent colleges too. All this gave him a deep understanding that **'YES'** a lot can be done in this field.

The **'journey to success'** began because this was the time when he accepted the business **'wholeheartedly.'**

He started attending all the meetings, never missed even a single session. Even in uncomfortable situations, he attended meetings.

He shares an experience that once he had to go for a meeting at 10 PM, it was the first year of college hostel; thus he was not allowed to leave. He requested a lot but all was in vain.

But Mr. Bhupendra was so passionate to go that he jumped off and escaped from the hostel. Despite of being hurt, he attended the full meeting.

It is said –

"I am going to succeed because I'm crazy enough to think I can."

This line fits into the attitude of Mr. Bhupendra. It's a successful person's mindset that he works wholeheartedly, even in the conditions that might be unfavorable to him.

A successful person has an attitude of converting adverse conditions to favorable.

One who keeps making excuses can never, ever achieve anything significant in life. Success comes to those who are dedicated and focused on their goals.

Very beautifully said by **Swami Vivekananda**,

"All power is within you."

Mr. Bhupendra Pal proved that –

'We can do anything and everything.'

He could have given an excuse for not attending that meeting, but he is far from reasons & excuses.

He found a way and completed his task. We must remember that we all have powers, but our negative belief system stops us. Each of us is full of infinite powers; only negative thinking prevents us from being successful.

First and foremost, the tip given by Mr. Bhupendra for becoming successful is –

"Be crazy to achieve your goals."

❦❦❦

THREE
Rejections to a source of Motivation

"Rejection gives me more power to work harder."

When he started showing business opportunity plans to friends, relatives, and other people, he got rejected by 47 people. A weak-minded person would have left this business, thinking that this business is not for him. But, Mr. Bhupendra is a very strong-minded person. He never stopped and kept working harder.

As **Robert Schuller**says,

"Tough Time never lasts, but Tough People do!"

Time never remains the same. We face failures in life, but strong-minded people never stop at challenging times. They keep giving their best, even in the worst time. Mr. Bhupendra gave an essential learning that we must implement in our life too. The rejections, he got after showing business opportunities, instead of getting demotivated, proved a factor of Motivation.

He said,

"Rejections gave me powers."

So, he never stopped and kept working even harder. His friends & relatives kept saying that –

"You cannot do this! You can never be successful."

He used these negative and demotivating statements as a fuel to his motivation and said to himself that –

NETWORK MARKETING - 'SLOW START TO SUPER SUCCESS'

"I have to prove them by achieving something big that they can't even imagine."

Thus rejections, objections, and challenges became his source of power.

Slowly and steadily attending all the meetings, learning more and more, Mr. Bhupendra understood network marketing's power and became successful in achieving from a

"Wrist-watch to BMW."

The main reason for his success is the consistency and faith that he developed on the power of network marketing. He never stopped and kept working even harder. Even after continuous rejections, he never looked back, kept on making new goals, and achieved them.

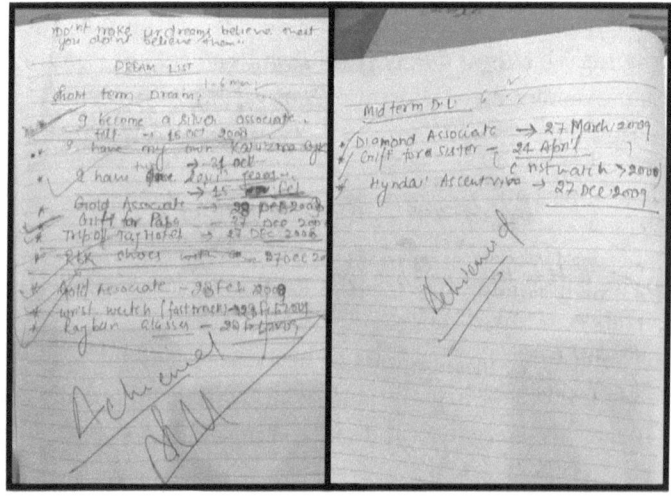

Diary pages of Mr.Bhupendra Pal

This way, he used to pen down his dreams and invests his full focus and dedication to achieve it.

He achieved all his dreams from -

'Fast Track wristwatch in 2009

To

BMW car in 2017'

▷▷▷

FOUR
WHAT 'NEXT'?

"After success or achievement, make the next goal immediately."

Mr. Bhupendra Pal never thought of stopping and relaxing after a success or achievement. When he achieves his target goal, he asks himself,

"What Next?"

And immediately makes his next higher goal and strives harder to achieve it. That's why even after getting from small to big achievements and massive successes, still Mr. Bhupendra is unstoppable.

He keeps on making new goals and works with full enthusiasm for achieving it. The quality of a leader is that he never stops. He keeps on making a new set of goals, and when he reaches there instead of staying there, he finds a higher point and work to achieve that higher goal.

The mistake that maximum people do is getting into a comfort zone after small achievements. We sit back and get relaxed when we get a fair amount of money in our account and some popularity and success.

We come to a state that we start taking things for granted and begin skipping meetings because we don't have our next goal or a bigger vision. We get relaxed, and our enthusiasm diminishes, and thus business fails.

But Mr. Bhupendra always keeps a bigger vision and remains enthusiastic.

As very beautifully quoted by

Mr. Gordon Parks-

"Enthusiasm is the electricity of life. How do you get it? You act enthusiastic until you make it a habit".

This quotation entirely fits in the case of Mr. Bhupendra, as he has always been enthusiastic. Enthusiasm is the power source; one cannot achieve big success until he is passionate about his work.

The most significant example of the most enthusiastic person is Mr. Sachin Tendulkar, who never stopped and attained higher and higher success.

Once in an interview, the interviewer asked Sachin Tendulkar about the -

"Secret of Success?"

'What made you strong and stable for such a long career four years of domestic cricket, and 20 years of international cricket?'

He said,

"Practice, I do practice for 12 hours a day. Every morning at 6 AM, I reach the ground with my pads on and start my Cricket."

Interviewer again asked –

"If you have made a century or a double century in the match. Then, what is your next day schedule? Are you eager to see the newspaper, TV, and social media of what compliments you got from your fans?"

Sachin Tendulkar replied,

"No, at 6 AM, I go to ground, and first play 500 balls. Then I open my social media."

This consistency in Practice and passion for Cricket made him achieve the nation's highest award –

'Bharat Ratna' and more than '1 billion fans' around the world.

Mr. Bhupendra Pal also teaches us that success becomes a disease if we get attached to it and stop working. Enjoy success, but only for a while, then immediately, we should start working towards the next goal. If you don't have the following plan, then there are chances of failure.

We all know Vinod Kambli, who is the best friend of Sachin Tendulkar. He was more talented than Sachin but failed miserably in Cricket.

Both friends of almost the same age. One failed, and another became 'Lord of Cricket' with a billion followers.

The reasons for his failure were -

- Lack of passion,
- Lack of attitude, and
- Lack of work ethics

These three are above all the talents.

That's why Mr. Bhupendra Pal says not to stop and relax. This Network Marketing business requires full passion and strong will.

Mr. Bhupendra Pal says,

"Business grows when we want to grow."

Willpower, a strong "why" and "What Next" -these are three principles according to him that can make any person achieve the highest success that one can dream.

The best thing about network marketing is the meetings that teach us and motivates us. So, Mr. Bhupendra Pal says,

"We must never miss any meeting."

He shared an experience - it was in starting when he had a small team of 10 people; they joined a company event.

In that event, the speaker said, "I have a network in four to five states and many colleges."

Mr. Bhupendra Pal got so much motivated, and a strong desire came in his mind, and he asked himself,

"Why can't I reach to his level ?"

He came back to the hostel room and took out a list of almost all North-India engineering colleges. He met his upline with the plan and told him that –

"In the next three years, we will have a network in every college of North India."

Now, this became the goal of his college life, and then he started living this goal. For this, he broke the barriers of excuses and went out, visited other colleges to make his dream come true.

"If your mind is full of with dreams, then there is no room for fear."

He became fearless and worked with full energy.

Like many great business people who started their journey from a small room office, garage, or hostel room, Mr. Bhupendra Pal also started his big network marketing business from a small hostel room. To do a big business, one cannot remain confined to a small area. One cannot limit himself.

So, Mr. Bhupendra Pal went out to the colleges found contacts and links. As a result of his dedication and hard work, the organization, which was a regional organization in 2008, within his college time in 2011, it became North India's largest organization of this field.

Mr. Bhupendra Pal admires college days a lot. He quotes, a dialogue of a movie "Rang De Basanti" in which Aamir Khan says –

"College de gate de is taraf hum life ko nachate hai te duji taraf life humko nachati hai."

It means we control life during college days, but the situations and circumstances control our lives after college life.

So message to all youngsters by Mr. Bhupendra Pal,

"Do such works that you should control your life rather than situations or circumstances control your life."

Mr. Bhupendra Pal, with great experience, has emerged as a live example for all the youngsters. Usually, youngsters, college students lack money. But he, even in college days, had no scarcity of money. He lived an extraordinary life throwing a party and lived a life that every college student dreams. And not a single penny was taken by his family. It was learned by himself. In college days, his monthly income reached in lakhs.

There was an instance that happened in seventh semester exam days, he gave his exam of subject Hydraulics in civil engineering, and unfortunately, he didn't do well in it, as he was not well prepared. He was quite upset after the exam. But after the exam, one thing, gave him a big smile on his face that was the mobile SMS notification 32,500/- credited amount in his account, and this was his weekly income.

Similarly, many instances took place in college life. In the third year of college, with his own money, he purchased a brand-new car and lived a luxurious life during college days.

▷▷▷

FIVE
Opting Network Marketing As A Full-Time Business

"Network Marketing is not just recruiting people, but it's about working on each of them to create a big network."

Mr. Bhupendra Pal completed his college in 2011, when his father called and asked him,

"What will you do now?"

He wanted Bhupendra to go to Delhi and prepare for UPSE and become a government employee.

But Mr. Bhupendra Pal wanted to continue with the business. Mr. Bhupendra Pal stated,

"If I do the job, I can contribute to my family and keep them happy, but if I will do network marketing, I can transform thousands of lives and I can contribute in their lives too."

So, in 2011, he took network marketing as a full-time profession.

After that, he worked to make his national presence.

He used to travel a lot. In 2013 the train compartment became his hotel room as he used to travel while sleeping from one city to another. In 2014, there was a time when in just 48 hours, Mr. Bhupendra Pal took 11 flights, Delhi to Bangalore, Bangalore to Chennai, Chennai to Delhi, and Delhi to Kolkata. On this hectic traveling, Mr. Bhupendra Pal says,

"I enjoyed it."

This hectic traveling became enjoyable for him, all because of his passion. He is very passionate about creating a big Network all around the country.

In 2015 first convention was held in the Thyagaraj Stadium where all the people of his organization, across the country, participated.

In 2016, also a convention was held in the Thyagaraj Stadium.

In 2017, a convention was held in the IGI.

In top colleges like IITs and NITs, almost all college youngsters have connected. After all these achievements, Mr. Bhupendra Pal has already started working on his next goal. That is to have the next convention at Jawaharlal Nehru Stadium, Delhi, by the year 2023.

In the next 3 to 4 years, he wants to touch, at least ten million families with organization products and services.

▷▷▷

SIX
WHY NETWORK MARKETING?

"Life which has a balance of both time and money is the real successful life."

Question -"Why network marketing?"

Answer – To attain financial & time freedom.

What is Financial freedom? –

They have enough residual income to cover living expenses. This financial freedom is different from person to person. A person might not feel financially free even with 100 crores, while another person might feel financially free with ten crores or one crore.

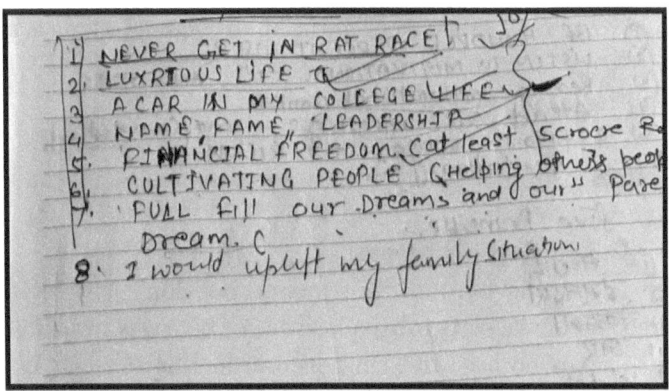

Image taken from Mr. Bhupendra Pal's diary of why he wanted to join network marketing.

Important eight reasons for joining network marketing by Mr. Bhupendra Pal were:-

- Never get in "Rat Race."
- Luxurious Life
- A car in college life

- Name & fame
- Financial Freedom
- Help others
- Fulfill personal & parent's dreams
- Uplift family

Another reason for why network marketing,

There are four types of people: -
   (Based on time and money)
   The first type of people–
   Work in an office from morning to evening, six days a week; do not have any time and money.
   The second type of people–
   Those people, who have time but have no money. Our country is full of such people; a lot of unemployed people are there in India.
   The third type of people–
   Those who have a lot of money, but don't have time freedom. A real story can explain this – There was a wealthy advocate who used to earn a lot but had no time for his family. One day, his daughter came to him and asked for a thousand bugs, the lawyer got a bit surprised still gave his wallet to her and said, "Take whatever you want." The daughter took a thousand bugs out of the wallet, and she went to her room and takes 500 bugs, added it to one thousand bugs, then came back to her father and gave 1500 bugs and said, "Papa, this is your fees, take it and give your one hour to me because I have heard your one-hour fee is 1500 bugs!". These are the type of people who have a lot of money, but no time.

Today, maximum parents are involved in their profession and business so much that they don't give time to their family. That's why today's children get into a bad company; spouse getting separated has become common. People earn lots of money getting all kinds of material success, but the family is getting spoiled. Getting all financial success on the cost of the family is a great loss. It is the biggest loss if bank accounts are full, but you're left with no one of your own to enjoy. It is not a successful life if financial success is there, but family relations are spoiled. So, such people have a lot of money, but scarcity of time leads to failure.

The fourth type of people–
Are those who have both time and money in balance.
Mr. Bhupendra Pal says, –

"If I want to spend a month out with my family, I can do that; I don't have to send mail to my boss or ask for a holiday, I am boss myself. While enjoying with my family, my bank account gets credited with my company payouts."

If you can do what you aspire and have enough money and time, you are financially free.

Therefore **Mr. Bhupendra Pal encourages a life with both time as well as financial freedom.**

Network Marketing is that platform in which if you work for four to five years regularly with consistency and create a big network of independent leaders, you can achieve a situation where you can relish both time and money.

Another reason for why network marketing,

There are three kinds of power: -

- **Power of position,**
- **Power of money,**
- **Power of association.**

The power of position includes prominent politicians & bureaucrats.

The power of money includes business leaders like Ambanis, Tata, and all they have a lot of money to do anything.

The power of association is the most significant. If we unite people for a common goal, then success can be achieved in much less time. This power of association is so high that it can cause constitutional amendments too.

In network marketing through your product services and education & training, a significant association can be created.

The best investment is not in real estate or share market, but the best investment is time because a person can grow more than real estate and more than the share market.

Network Marketing is a platform where your success depends on other's success. If you develop people, try to bring positive changes in their lives and succeed.

Mr. Bhupendra Pal says,

"I love to help people by bringing value addition and positive change in their life."

> *"Developing people and making them successful is directly proportional to your success."*

Network marketing is an opportunity in which we get a chance to make positive changes in the lives of the masses.

Another reason of "why network marketing."

There are two sources of income –

- **Active source**
- **Passive source**

In network marketing, we have to create a network of people. Then this network works for us, and we get freedom of both time and money.

Let's understand ESBI is a concept of earning money.

E – Employ

S – Self-employed,

B – Business

I – Investor

In network marketing, a simple middle-class person can jump from a self-employed zone to set up a business, and, through business, he can become an investor.

Network Marketing gives an average earning self-employed middle-class person the opportunity to set up a big business. After making money through trade, he can become an investor. It is an excellent platform for ordinary people who make much money to invest in starting up in business.

With a low, almost negligible investment, a person can start a business, and there is no risk at all.

Therefore, this is the best opportunity.

It is an excellent platform for those who want to come in the business category. Also, comparing it to traditional business network marketing is much better as there is no risk because not much investment is required. Still, in traditional business, there is a lot of initial investment. Many established companies failed due to government policies or changes in market trends; the business got affected, and all the investment became zero. In network marketing, there is no chance of loss. Even if one couldn't do well and earn a fair amount of money in network marketing and benefit from the development, they get through network marketing's educational and training system.

Another reason of "why network marketing."

Network marketing makes us learn and grow in many dimensions because network marketer gets to work in various fields –

- **Sales,**
- **Marketing,**
- **Managing events,**
- **HR.**

The public speaking skills and communication skills, which are crucial in this 21st century, network marketers teach them all free of cost.

Unlike other professions, network marketing is a profession that allows us to grow in multiple fields. We grow in sales, marketing and leadership, organizational management, and people management. Thus, network marketing is the only field that provides a chance to flourish in many dimensions.

If we compare network marketing with other professions, a person who is in sales and marketing in some company remains in sales and marketing for a lifetime. But network marketers get a chance to explore and grow in other fields too.

Another reason of "why network marketing."

In network marketing, we learn various business skills, which help us to groom from both inside as well as outside. After learning these skills, we can do well in network marketing, but we can do other startup business too with better productivity. In all the business selling is expected, we sell products, ideas, and thoughts. This technique of selling is taught very nicely in network marketing at zero cost.

We get to learn skills of how to influence people, and we learn management skills and leadership skills.

People spend thousands and lakhs of money to learn business skills, but even after learning, people make mistakes and lose money in their business. But in network marketing with proper theoretical education, we can get practical learning through field experience. Unlike traditional business, network marketing has a team of people who help us support us to grow. At every step, guidance and education is available. But in traditional business, there is a cut through competition of being the best.

In network marketing, the growth depends on each other. Therefore, people help each other.

Many organizations exist online and offline in which business leadership skills, sales and marketing skills, management skills, and all business education is available. We like the atmosphere as the speakers deliver lectures on the topics very well. Motivation and inspiration are also given there through examples and stories. But the problem comes in the actual implementation of skills taught in the course. When some practical problem arises at ground level, the organization's theoretical education doesn't guide us and takes us out. They give all the theory education, but the practical implementation is missing. But in network marketing, we get day to day mentorship from our up-line and leaders. So many challenges come at ground level. But our up-line helps us give inspiration and motivation, but they also allow us to tackle all the small- significant challenges and problems that we face.

According to the book, **Copycat Marketing,** your income is directly proportional to your abilities and skills multiplied by working hours.

Some workaholic people work for 13 to 14 hours, but maximum people work for 8 to 10 hours, not more than that. But in network marketing, as Mr. Bhupendra says,

"I can work for 4000 to 10,000 hours in a day, just by working for one hour."

A network marketer can increase their number of working hours from 100 to 1000, 1000 to 10,000 per the team's size. Thus, as the number of team members increases, the number of working hours increases, and the income increases.

In Corporate, we get a good salary, but the income gets stagnated after a certain level. As we see, current time situations and jobs are not secure, whereas, in network marketing, payment generates to any extent, and there is no word like job security as we are our boss. Thus, we have time flexibilities too.

Emotional power is also essential for a business because everyone teaches us how to succeed, but very few people tell us how to handle failures. Failure causes a lot of stress and even results in depression. In traditional business, if a setback comes, we have very few people to support us, but in network marketing, we have many people to help even in challenging situations.

As it happened with Mr. Bhupendra Pal,

In the very beginning, almost 46 rejections he had to face, there was a situation that his own best friend, his childhood friend, rejected his proposal for which he traveled 500 kilometers from Lucknow to Ghaziabad.

All this rejection resulted in emotional issues, but he says,

"I got right up-line who helped me and encouraged me by saying, now you have to prove everyone wrong by achieving the highest success. So I did."

Network marketing is a good platform that makes us emotionally healthy. Also, it teaches us financial management and makes us spiritual. Positivity comes in our life.

Again, coming to the point discussed in starting, network marketing gives both time and financial freedom.

Mr. Bhupendra tells about his experience that he was not working for the company when he was in Mauritius for 15 to 20 days. He was utterly enjoying with his family.

Even then, his account got credited with 15 lakhs.

The power of network marketing that Mr. Bhupendra has created a strong team and independent leaders who work and generate income for him.

This tension-free work with enjoyment is experienced only by network marketers. Even prominent business people don't share this tension-free life. They are filled with tensions even when they are out for traveling with their family. They keep on checking reports guiding employers on the phone; their mind is fully occupied, even in the leisure time. But the network marketers are free from all types of tensions as they have created a network of independent leaders now; they take care of the business.

As said by Mr. Bhupendra Pal, the life of a successful network marketer is –

"Work for every 15 days and enjoy remaining 15 days of a month".

This lifestyle can be lived only by network marketers.

The only thing is a commitment to hard work in starting three to four years. After this, business gets into automatic mode.

But in traditional business, struggles & tensions remain a lifetime. There is no peace of mind. A luxurious life with a peace of mind can be achieved only in network marketing.

There are so many millionaires in Chandani Chowk, running a wholesale business on a large scale, they have a massive turnover of 5-10 crores, but the life is full of stress & tensions.

Even though they are earning a lot, but still, their life is not inspiring. No one wants to live such a life that has no peace of mind. Peace of mind in today's time is essential. Network Marketing is a platform that allows us to make a balance in time and money.

Another reason of "why network marketing."

Personality Development - The personal growth that we get in network marketing is tremendous. There is a 360-degree transformation of personality in network marketing.

There was a vast transformation in the life of Mr. Bhupendra Pal, before joining the Network Marketing Company, he says,

"I was completely zero, and communication skills were almost nothing. I was only good at studies that I got admission in IET Lucknow, and my personality was a big zero. My schooling was from the Hindi medium school of a small village. But network marketing proved a blessing to me, and my personality transformed at 360 degrees. Now I am a confident speaker, and I have developed an ability to speak on stage in front of thousands of people without fear or hesitation. Even the body language and looks also transformed from a villager to a professional networker. Thus, I recommend network marketing to everyone."

Today, we see so many great public speakers who can influence the masses. They all are directly or indirectly connected to network marketing.

To conclude, if we want to achieve something big in life, not only in terms of money, but also in terms of personality, popularity, and lifestyle, we must all do network marketing.

༄༄༄

SEVEN

WHY SHOULD WOMEN DO NETWORK MARKETING?

"Women, especially housewives, have a common question that they should do network marketing or not?"

Before answering this question, other related questions arise......

- Women especially housewives, don't have dreams?
- Don't they have any right to live with pride and honor in this society?
- Are they meant only for household works?

Unfortunately, a woman in India is still considered as the one made for household works only!

Isn't it good that woman too starts this business from her own house itself? Instead of being financially dependent on family, she becomes economically free and a financial contributor to the family?

Woman can get many benefits through this network marketing Business: -

- Good income

- She can fulfill her small and big dreams which are initially suppressed under family pressure.

- She can be able to give financial support to her family.

- There is time freedom in this business; thus, when women are free from household works. They can devote their free time to this business.

- As network marketing gives both name and fame in this field, women can earn more than any other family member.

The best thing of network marketing is the training that they give.

In traditional business, no one teaches -

"What and how to do?"

But in network marketing, the up-line is always present to guide us at every step. They tell us which action to take and how to take it. Network marketing is full of good people who are successfully building their businesses and helping others develop their business.

Thus, women can take the help of a successful up line and make their future bright.

Network Marketing not only helps in making a good income, but it transforms the personality that a woman couldn't even imagine. It improves both outer as well as inner being. The communication skills and the self-confidence reach to the next level.

Thus, network marketing is the right choice for a woman, which gives confidence and financial stability.

EIGHT

Why do students need "network marketing"?

"College going Students, have a common question that they should do network marketing or not?"

- **Do students adopt network marketing?**
- **Won't it affect their studies?**
- **Won't it create disturbance in their studies?**

Before answering this question. A question for all of us –

After school or College, when students come back, don't they spend hours and hours on social media, wasting their time on Face book, WhatsApp, and other platforms?

When students turn 18, won't they have their own needs?

They want money to buy phone, throw parties, etc. They don't like asking for money from family, now and then. Many expenses increase in their life at this age.

Thus, for income and self-dependency, students must join network marketing.

In fact, in western countries, maximum families leave their kids when they turn 15 or 16 years of age. They sponsor themselves for higher studies and start making money of their own by doing jobs or some business.

There are many benefits for students in Network Marketing -

- For small-small expenses of their own, they won't have to trouble their parents.
- They will use the present time properly, which they used to waste on social media. On average, 16 to 24 years of students spend three to four hours on social media. Now, instead of wasting time on social media, they will get the best use of it by growing their business on social media.
- Also, at this age, students are promoted to College for further studies. There are chances of getting them into bad company. But when they are with network marketing, they get a healthy environment full of inspiration & guidance of cheerful people who allow them to earn name and fame in their lives.
- We all know, getting into an engineering college or any other system & earning a degree is easy. But regarding the current situation of the market, there is less or no

jobs. Only that student succeeds who already have the experience of doing some business in their college time.
- After College, students can opt for network marketing as their full-time career as done by Mr. Bhupendra Pal.

Mr. Bhupendra Pal joined network marketing in the 2008 first year of his College. In the initial pages, we have already read that how well he did this business in college days with studies, he made an extensive network and lakhs of income, and lived a great college life with no scarcity of money.

He stopped taking money from his family after the second year and became financially independent. He bought his first car with his own money. And after he passed in 2011, he opted for network marketing as a full-time business. And today, we all know how much he is successful in this business.

The network marketing industry has time freedom and the potential to make anyone a **"millionaire"**. It depends on the person how he or she takes this business.

It is a 100% risk-free business as it has no loss, and students usually lack savings so they can join a network marketing company for free or with little investment. With hard work and patience, they can earn lots of money, but they can also groom their personalities thoroughly.

Thus, students must do Network Marketing.

▷▷▷

NINE

WHAT ARE THE COMMON MISTAKES? HOW TO AVOID AND CORRECT THEM?

"There is no secret of success there is only a system of success."

First mistake –

The biggest mistake that we do is that we don't follow the system but try to find a short-cut secret to success in network marketing. Mr. Bhupendra Pal says,

> ***"There is no secret of success; there is only a system of success".***

If we follow the system and work whole-heartedly, we will succeed for sure.

Second mistake –

It is said that **'boss is always right.'** Similarly, in Network Marketing me must consider our active growing up-line as our Boss. We make mistake by ignoring our up-line. In fact, we try to judge him; we find faults in our own team and up-lines. But we must always remember that our up-line is always right, so to attain success we should never doubt the mentorship & guidance of the up-line.

Mr. Bhupendra Pal says,

> ***"I was not afraid of my father as much as of my up-line."***

This was the level of respect & fear that he had for his up-line.

Third mistake –

Our up-line always asks us to make a list of potential members, but we don't make it. We think we have the contact list and avoid making it on pen and paper.

We must understand that proper planning of potential members is essential. We must schedule the date & time, accordingly we should meet them.

Fourth mistake -

We don't work for our self-development.

Our up-line keeps telling us to read books, listen to audios, and see motivational and educational training videos, but we avoid it, which affects our business.

Rejections arise due to the lack of proper skills and knowledge, our productivity increases when we train ourselves with regular intake of the company's knowledge and skills.

We become confident to answer difficult questions and become emotionally strong to handle rejections.

Fifth mistake –

We don't attend the company's meetings & events regularly.

"Events act as a catalyst that strongly connects us to our business"

(Said by Mr. Bhupendra Pal)

He also shared his experience that he was not working for almost three months in starting because he wasn't attending any event when he joined network marketing.

But when he attended his first event, he saw so many people who were so successful, that it became a turning moment of his life.

Mr. Bhupendra Pal says,

"Joining network marketing was never a turning moment for me but, attending my first event was a turning moment of my life. I opted for network marketing seriously, only

after attending that event."

But people make mistakes by missing events by making excuses.

This way, the business gets affected.

Mr. Bhupendra Pal says,

"If you miss one event or meeting, some gap comes between you and your business, but when you ignore all events continuously for one month, you are away from your business."

Thus, we must take the company events & meetings very seriously and try not to miss any session.

Sixth mistake –

We forget not only our actions are duplicated, but our mindset is also duplicated. When our thought process is contaminated with negativity continuously then after some time it starts to reflect in our behavior. Our negative thoughts and our views, shared by us to others, spread like a Chinese whisper from one person to another. Thus the contamination of our mind affects the whole organization.

As it is rightly said,

'Negativity' gets promoted faster than positivity.

Thus, we must maintain the right mindset to get the right kind of thoughts.

Seventh mistake –

When our words and actions are not in synchronization. We are asking our down-line to follow the system, but we ourselves are not following it, then this is not a good leadership quality. A leader must be a role model for others. He must follow his words then ask others to follow.

Eighth mistake –

We join network marketing with big aspirations, but we don't work hard to achieve it. We get into comfort zone after getting small achievements; we don't remain motivated throughout the journey.

Mr. Bhupendra Pal says,

> **"I couldn't have achieved BMW from a small wristwatch if I stopped, but I always had a 'What Next!' factor in my mind, which keeps me motivated."**

Similarly, we all must have an inspiration that keeps us charged and energetic, not allowing failures and achievements to stop our path of success. Once we achieve the short term goal then immediately we must start working to attain the long term goal i.e to become a top earner.

Ninth mistake –

When we achieve some success, we bring three diseases - First-arrogance, Second - inefficiency. Third - complacency. Worst of all is 'arrogance.' The problem of ego arises with success. This is one of the biggest mistakes that network marketers do when they achieve success.

But Mr. Bhupendra Pal says,

"As you achieve more success, more humbleness and simplicity should come in your life."

Otherwise, when success results in ego, then downfall comes." Thus, the quality of simplicity and humbleness is a must.

Tenth mistake –

The communication gap between you and your up-line. This factor also affects business. Communication gap can be of some information of policy change or some product launch, or rates revision. This kind of essential data should be communicated with the team on time. Else, this communication gap might become very harmful to the business.

Eleventh mistake –

Since there is no boss in network marketing; therefore, people take this business for granted. Thus, the resultant outcomes of the company are also significantly less. Consequently,

Mr. Bhupendra Pal says,

"If you don't have a boss, then make your up-line as your boss, to whom you can follow with full dedication."

We must make our growing active up-line as our mentor and our boss and then observe what transformation comes to our business.

Twelfth mistake–

Some leaders don't plan a proper schedule.

Mr. Bhupendra Pal says,

"Planning a proper schedule and then following it is very important because it inspires and motivates us to work."

Proper scheduling makes our time fully utilized and organized.

Thirteenth mistake –

Some people are narrow-minded. They try to remain enclosed in a single place or zone. They don't think of developing a network or business in other sites. We must not limit to a single place or area; we can build our network throughout the country.

Fourteenth mistake –

We consider network marketing as a sales business. This is a business, in which sales is a component. We make a mistake by only concentrating on sales. By being a salesman, a person can make two to three sales per day, not more than that.

But if we focus on creating networks & developing them by giving them proper training, education, thousands of deals can be done in a day, with a strong system. People do a mistake by just concentrating on joining new associates and after that, they forget them.

We must remember that joining is just like 'planting a seed.' It won't grow if we are not nurturing it. This nurturing of the team is very integral.

Regular conversation, regular guidance is very important to make the team inspired and strong. A group of 10 active team members are better than - '1000 inactive team' members.

Therefore, we must make sure that the team and we are to be trained with the necessary skills discussed incoming chapter.

Above all are the common mistakes that a networker must avoid on the path of success in the network marketing business.

TEN

Importance of Strong Character In Network Marketing

"Character and faith is the base of network marketing"

If you want to be successful in network marketing, you need to imbibe all the qualities of a successful leader.

Most essential quality that makes a person a successful leader is the **'character.'**

In network marketing, we need to work on both character and skills. A person might have tremendous skills for invitation, presentation, follow up, and objection handling. Such a person can make a fantastic team. But he can't sustain it for long if he doesn't have a strong character.

There are many examples of highly educated people who have extraordinary skills, but they perform average in the network marketing business. Whereas, people with almost no skills in starting, but with a strong character, performed excellently in the network marketing business.

Because strong character makes us

- More accountable, and
- Responsible

Having this quality, even a less skilled person, can create a substantial business. Many up-lines commit big mistakes by treating their down-line as employees, whereas the person with the right character never shows boss nature to anyone. They treat the team as their own family members. So they give a lot of love, care, and respect to everyone in their team.

Some people try to create fast money using unfair practices or unethical practices. They try to build their business by using people. They think of only their selfish benefits.

This nature might give them temporary success, which never lasts for long, whereas, a person with strong character always uses business to build people. He thinks of the growth of other people, more than himself.

Maximum people fail in network marketing, not because of skills and talent; they fail because of a weak character.

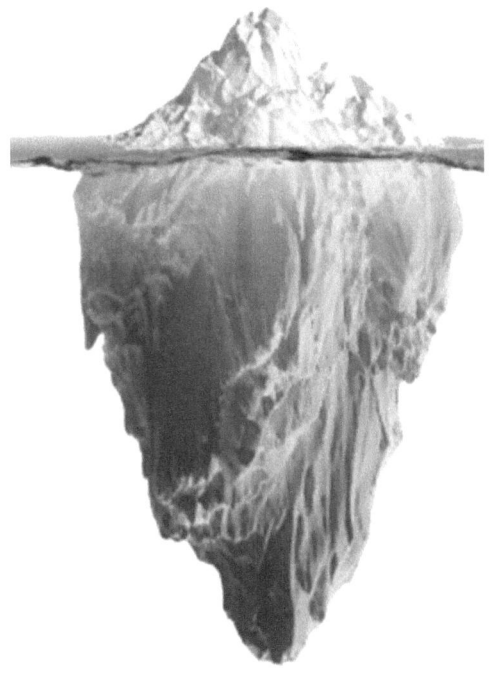

Iceberg

Let's understand with an example of an iceberg.

As we know, the iceberg looks too small from outside. But from inside, it is huge and massive.

If we see the small visible part of the iceberg as skills, then the part immersed in water, which is invisible to our eyes, is the character.

Character is not visible, but it is the foundation stone of our business. We need to become a good human being first with the mentality that we don't work with machines, we are working with people.

So, without being the right person, how can we lead them?

So, to become a person with a strong character, we need to cultivate the following values.

- **Honesty,**
- **Truthfulness,**
- **Kind heartedness,**
- **Generosity,**
- **Patience,**
- **Love, and**
- **Respect**

In this business, we must aim towards the growth of other people around us. For this, we need to develop the above values. The most important is love in our hearts for different people. We cannot uplift others by scolding, hatred, etc.

To develop skills - education and training system is to be followed. But to build character, we need to define various principles and values of our life. So when we develop principles and values like love, truthfulness, honesty, etc. Then we move towards becoming a good human being, which is most important for success.

Strong character makes us win the hearts of other people.

A person with strong character always –

- **Follows ethics and values**

- **Has right intention**

- **Is responsible and**

- **Has a similarity in words and actions.**

- **He doesn't give only lectures, but teaches with his actions.**

ppp

ELEVEN
Essential Skills to Become Successful in Network Marketing

"To become successful in Network Marketing, we need to surrender to our mentor or guru."

Introduction

No special skills are required to join Network Marketing, but we must develop specific skills to attain success.

One can start with zero, but gradually skills are required to be learned, which are necessary to succeed.

"Opening Shop is not enough; you must learn Shop-keeping."

People spend years & years working hard, but they don't work on their self-development.

Mr. Bhupendra Pal says that he wasn't from any business background. Therefore, he had almost no skills, but he realized the importance of various skills after joining Network marketing. He started training himself by learning those skills from the experts of their company.

He says,

"I was never good at sales. But after I realized the importance, then I started learning all skills like – invitation, presentation, closing, follow-up & objection handling. Learning these skills boosted my network marketing carrier to another level."

Essential skills in network marketing include: -

- **Invitation**
- **Presentation**
- **Follow-up**
- **Doubt Clearing or Objection Handling.**

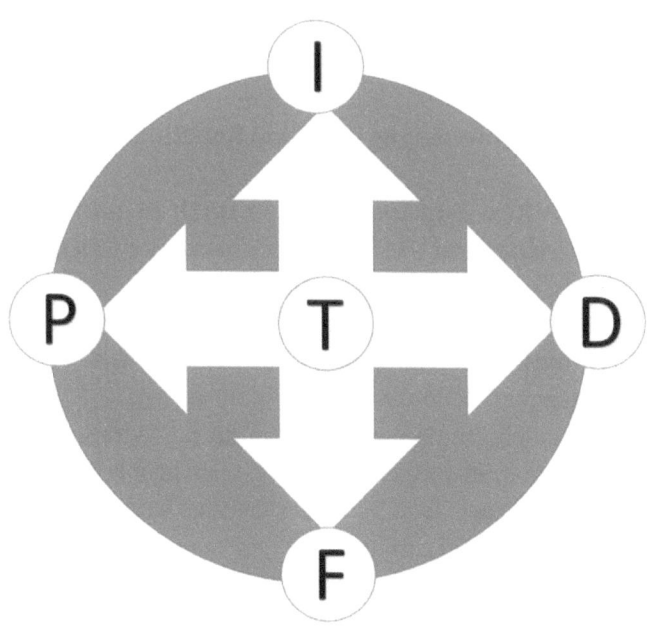

Wheel of freedom

Wheel of Freedom

"One who learns the art of rotating the 'Wheel of freedom'

Attains the highest Network Marketing success"

(© Mr. Nikhil Pratap Singh)

T = TRAINING
I = Invitation
P = Presentation
F = Follow-Up
D = Doubt Clearing or Objection Handling

> ## *"When any work we do with proper knowledge and skills, then chances of success increase to maximum."*

The most significant power of any country is the youth population of that country.

Fortunately, India has a maximum percentage of the youth population. India is a country full of people below the age of 35. This age, 18 to 35, is very creative, and also people are full of energy at this age.

All the successful people used this age of their life span to the fullest. They developed their skills, habits, and personality.

This utilization of golden years made them extraordinary and achieved many milestones in their life.

This age of 18 to 35 is crucial too, as maximum youth get diverted to worldly attractions and forget their goals.

Therefore, on the one hand, this segment of youth has the most significant power. On the other hand, it can prove to be a big disaster if not channelized properly.

If proper channelization is not given to the youth, they can prove to be our country's biggest weakness.

One of the most significant issues in our country is unemployment as jobs are reducing day by day. India's youth is becoming jobless.

Mr. Bhupendra Pal says,

"Biggest solution to unemployment is network marketing, which changes the mindset of job seeker to job creator."

Every person on this earth is born with some talent. All have a creative mind. Therefore, if we understand our talent and try to attain some essential skills, success can be achieved. Every person has the potential to become successful.

Network marketing is a platform that allows us to unleash talents. It will enable us to learn the 21st century's necessary skills which play a vital role in almost every business.

Network marketing provides an opportunity for an ordinary person to become an extraordinary person.

Any person, with or without any skill, can join network marketing.

Network marketing has a system that provides education and training to emphasize skills and knowledge to people.

When any work we do with proper knowledge and skills, then chances of success increase to maximum.

The coming chapters include the detailed explanation of the basic skills.

❦❦❦

TWELVE
Invitation Skills

SUPREET BATRA

"Curiosity, Gravity and Benefit are the important fundamentals of Invitation"

Important fundamentals of invitation:-

- *Curiosity,*

- *Gravity, and*

- *Benefit.*

Let us understand with an example.

Mr. Ram is a network marketer who wants to invite his friend, Mr. Sharma, to join his company.

Here, Mr. Sharma has not much knowledge of this industry.

Mr. Ram will start with general talks like,

"Hello Sharma ji, how are you? How's your work?" and all.

After similar general talks, Mr. Ram will say,

"Have you heard about this 21st century fastest growing business?" (With this line, Mr. Ram brought some **curiosity** to know more about the business and implanted a question in Mr. Sharma.)

When Mr. Sharma asks, "What is this business? Please tell."

Then the conversation, which was just informal in starting, becomes an invitation of network marketing business opportunity.

Now the next line of Mr. Ram will be,

"Oh, you haven't heard about this business. It is a very trending business, which has made so many people to achieve both financial and time freedom." (This way, Mr. Ram gave more **gravity** (weightage) to his conversation.)

Further Mr. Ram says, "This is a platform in which any common man can achieve his dreams."(This way, he added **the benefit** of opting for this business to his conversation.)

Thus by adding **Curiosity, Gravity, and Benefit** to the conversation will implant interest in Mr. Sharma's mind.

Then he will ask for further details.

Then, Mr. Ram can finally invite him to show business opportunities.

In general conversation itself, seeing an appropriate time, we can easily invite anyone using the fundamentals of invitation skills, i.e. curiosity, gravity, and benefit.

Types of the 'Ways of Invitation':-

1.
   Direct Invitation

2.
   Indirect Invitation

Direct Invitation

Direct Invitation includes the name of the network marketing industry

For Example, A Network Marketer can ask,

"Have you heard about network marketing?"

"Do you know what direct selling is?"

"This is India's biggest employment, providing industry, which has made thousands of millionaires."

Direct Invitation starts with an immediate question based on Network Marketing or Direct Selling and continues with the benefits of network marketing or direct selling industry.

Direct Invitation is for those who are close to us like our family, relatives & friends.

Indirect Invitation

There are multiple ways of Indirect Invitation. Here, we don't use the name of the network marketing industry in the starting. But we start the Invitation by telling the benefits of the industry.

There are so many people in our circle who are struggling with time and money. Some people have a lot of time, but no money, whereas others have money, but no time.

Every person has either some financial or time issues.

Therefore, we can tell them that there is an opportunity to solve their issues related to time & money.

This opportunity can lead us to achieve both time and financial freedom.

It will make people ask for further knowledge as no one likes a 9 to 5 job. And also, no one is satisfied with only one source of income. Therefore, for sure, people will accept our Invitation to know more about the business opportunity.

Mr. Robert Kiyosaki famous economist says, there are two types of income –

- *Active income, and*

- *Passive income*

As we all know, active income is an income we get when we work for it.

Passive income is the income that we get even when we are not actively working for it.

We can ask people (prospects) –

"Do you have any source of passive income along with your active income?"

Maximum people will say "No" as they are dependent only on an active source of income. They don't have any passive income sources.

Then we can tell them that there is a business opportunity, which can take them to the passive income category. It will empower people, and make them more curious. Therefore, an Invitation to the business plan executes.

Another way to invite –
We can ask,

"Do you want to be your own boss?"

There is a vast percentage of people who are not at all satisfied with their jobs. They work only to fulfill their essential needs. They listen to the boss's scolding and tolerate his dominance.

When we offer them that "you can become your own boss," this line attracts people as many of them are upset with their jobs and they don't have time freedom. For family outings, they keep struggling to get holiday.

Also, in today's time, jobs are no more secure source of income.

Therefore, when we tell them the above reasons, people get curious about knowing 'how to become one's own boss.'

This way, we can invite them for the business opportunity presentation.

Another way of Invitation......
We can ask –

"When you're planning your retirement?"

When we ask this question to 35 to 40 years of age group, they get surprised because maximum people still think that the retirement age is 60 to 65.

This curiosity about getting financial retirement at an early age makes them ask – 'How?'

Then we can tell them that we have a business opportunity. In which, by working from five to six years, we can achieve financial freedom, and therefore we can plan an early retirement.

Every person wants to enjoy life with family & friends, but the golden years of life experience get wasted in Job.

People get attracted by the idea of early retirement by becoming financially free.

So they ask -

'How we can achieve financial freedom?' or 'How can we plan, an early retirement?'

This excitement will allow us to invite them to the business opportunity presentation.

Another way of Invitation.....

Every person has some or the other problem. If we can address their situation with a suitable solution, this also becomes a way of Invitation.

We can do Invitation or prospect building by showing or presenting a set of benefits of network marketing.

Another way of Invitation......

We can ask,

"Do you want to earn extra income?"

We can tell "an extra income can be earned by investing two to three hours per day without quitting a job or running business."

We can say that "this business opportunity can increase your overall income by 20 25%, just by giving two to three hours per day." And if you work continuously, then this can give you a complete financial solution.

So, this also becomes a way of invitation.

Another way of Invitation......

To invite college students, we can ask:-

- "Do you want to be self-dependent and pay your fees yourself?" "Do you want to buy a bike with your own money?"
- "Do you want to get name and fame at an early age?"
- "Do you want to learn entrepreneur skills?"

When student agrees to any of these questions, then we can invite them to the business opportunity.

Therefore to conclude,

Prospect building can be done by using fundamentals of Invitation –

1. Curiosity,
2. Gravity,
3. Benefits and a
4. Also by both direct and indirect ways of invitation.

THIRTEEN
OBJECTION HANDLING SKILLS

"Maximum objections occur because of wrong mindset"

When we present the business opportunity to people, we have to face multiple questions and objections.

Today's people are full of myths and fears because of incomplete knowledge of network marketing.

Objection handling or doubt clearing is nothing but removing the myths and doubts and presenting the real picture of network marketing.

70 To 75% of genuine prospects ask four to five questions before joining. Answering the questions is an essential skill.

For developing this Objection handling skill, the following points must be followed:-

Firstly, we must develop a habit of listening,

Listening is essential. The problem of most of the conversation is that we don't listen to the other person.

So, we must listen appropriately to the needs, requirements, and doubts of the prospect.

Secondly, be courageous,

We shouldn't get afraid of doubts or objections, because doubts and objections only come when the prospect seems interested in the business opportunity.

Four major categories of questions or objections

- **Money issues**
- **Time issues**
- **Relatives and family issues**
- **Self-doubt**

These are four major categories of questions or objections that we, as network marketers, have to handle.

Now, how to handle these objections?

There are three essential tools to handle all kinds of objections.

Concept - Triple F

- F(Feel)
- F(Felt)
- F(Found)

First objection related to money issues.

Objection: - "I don't have money to invest in this business opportunity."

Reply of network marketer can be:-
"Not having money is an achievement or problem?"
"Of course it's a problem,"
"Since it's a problem, we must find a solution for it."
Then use the **concept of 'Feel-Felt-Found'**
"See, what you **feel** today, I also **felt** the same few months or years back. But then I thought it is a small investment that gives me products in return and an opportunity to solve my financial problems.

Thus, I opted for the business, and now I have started earning money through it."

We can also give examples of our up-lines, who earns a good amount and have achieved financial freedom.

We may tell the statics of network marketing, but people won't connect as they believe only in realities.

According to the concept of 'Feel-Felt-Found.'

'What do you feel? I felt the same.'

We have to show people that you and I are the same.

People only like to talk to those who understand their mindset.

So, we must talk to them by coming to their level of mind. In this way, the chances of prospect to client conversion increases.

Second objection related to time issues

Objection: - "I can't manage this business with my job. I don't have time".

Using the concept of 'Feel-Felt-Found'

We as a Network marketer can say-

"I also faced the same problem that how to manage between job and network marketing business. As this business doesn't need much time. So, I thought to utilize my free time and accepted this as a part-time business. Now I can say that I took the right decision. I am learning new skills, developing personality, and earning extra income too."

"I am getting the opportunity to learn skills like communication marketing, sales presentation. These are the 21st century's most important skills that we get to learn for free from the system of education and training and network marketing."

Third Objection because of wrong mind-set

Some people will have objections because they had some bad experiences in the past. For such people, we can explain through an example- A person who has never eaten 'samosa' in his life. For the first time, he orders samosa from a shop, and unfortunately, the filling of it was old (not fresh). So, this affected the digestion of that person. Now, the person has become so negative for samosa, due to this bad experience. But in reality, samosa is not the problem. The root cause is its wrong preparation.

The same is with network marketing-

Some people faced terrible experiences and became negative for the entire network marketing industry.

For such people, we need to present the right picture of network marketing. We need to convince them, telling that all network-marketing companies are not the same. Because of the few companies, we shouldn't make a wrong mindset for the whole industry. Thus by revealing the network marketing benefits, one can remove the old myths and concepts from the prospect's mind.

Some people come with very high expectations because of the wrong picture created by network marketers before them. They saw luxury cars, a lavish lifestyle and all, but in reality, you need to work for it. People have objections because they heard that they would get Audi, BMW in a few months, but this is a myth.

We must tell our prospects that network marketers require proper skills, education, and training. Then working for a few years with full dedication and thus, creating a big network of independent leaders, he can achieve success.

Network marketing is based on ethics and the right values. We must join people by presenting them with a clear picture that both hard and smart work is required for a few years in network marketing. But yes, once a huge network is made, then a lot of money can be earned without much effort.

A good network marketer never says,

"You don't have to work."

He always says,

"A lot of work is required in network marketing, but I am there with you, and we'll work together and achieve success."

The network marketing industry has the potential to make people successful and earn both name and fame, but the only problem is people don't work in the right way.

When we remove the doubts and objections of such people and show them the right direction with a clear picture of network marketing, prospects not only converts to associates but also become a good leader and work with full dedication and enthusiasm.

Success requires a clear mindset without any doubt.

Thus by the above tips, we can enhance our objection handling skills.

ᗅᗅᗅ

FOURTEEN
Presentation Skills

> ***"A good presenter makes his speech or presentation interesting by adding humor to it."***

Key ingredients of a good presentation include the following factors:-

1. **Decent dress up-**

    It plays a vital role as it affects personality.
    Every personality has **the concept of 'LAW.'**
    L - 'Looks'
    A - 'Actions'
    W - 'Words'
    In network marketing, personality plays an important role.
    Because in this business, people invest in the person who shows the business opportunity.
    They see the personality of the network marketer before they know the company's headquarter.
    Therefore, Looks, Actions & Words are essential.
    Looks include- what dress the network marketer is wearing, his hairstyle etc.
    Actions include- How we shake hands, how we sit, how we represent ourselves.
    Words include- The sentences we speak in one-on-one meetings, group meetings, and seminars. Therefore Looks, Actions, and Words affect personality ultimately.
    The best part of the network marketing system is that even an average-looking person can enhance his personality when he joins network marketing.

So, for a fair presentation, one must enhance his personality by learning skills through the network marketing company's education and training system.

2. **Confidence –**

Even the best product and best business opportunity gets rejected when delivering its presentation with 'low confidence.' Because confidence is the indication of how much knowledge and faith we have in our business.

A Network Marketer who has full faith in business never lacks confidence. He is always enthusiastic to show business plan with full confidence.

3. **Eye Contact -**

It is an essential part of body language. As we know that 'our eyes speak, even more than our words.'

Therefore in our presentation or eye contact with the listener should be proper.

4. **Body Language–**

In network marketing or any business, connecting to people is very important. Therefore, when presenting our business opportunity, our body language must be robust and lively.

Body language must reflect our confidence, faith, and dedication towards our network marketing business. It helps our learners to connect better.

Therefore, the proper way to express ourselves through facial expressions and gestures is essential to learn and to give an excellent presentation.

5. **Fluency –**

Fluency plays a vital role in the presentation. Oral fluency should be very smooth and precise, without many pauses.

Therefore, the ability to speak fluently is vital for becoming a better presenter or communicator.

6. **Language –**

We must see in which language we are comfortable.

If we are right in the Hindi language, then we must use this language to communicate.

Language also depends on the listener to whom we have to connect. At times we try to become very formal using formal words. But, if we want to relate better to the listener, we must talk in his language.

Because the listener doesn't invest in the plan or product, he invests in the presenter's personality.

Therefore, the presenter must use easy and amicable language so that listener gets connected easily.

7. **Voice Modulation –**

The vital point for any presentation is Voice Modulation.

It can make a simple presentation to an excellent presentation.

Every presenter must use voice modulation, like increasing voice, while speaking on the critical word to emphasize more.

By stressing more on tone words pitch, even a boring presentation can become very, very interesting.

8. **Humour–**

A good presenter makes his speech or presentation interesting by adding humor to it.

Humor and honesty are some of the essential attributes of a person.

To catch the attention of listeners, we must use humor as per the situation. It shouldn't be disrespecting to any person.

Humor is a language that everyone can understand. As we know that, when we share a 'laugh' with someone, we get connected to that person.

Therefore, the presentation can be made exciting and more engaging if we use a few situational humors. It can connect people with more focus. Also, it will make the presentation more enjoyable.

So these are eight main points for making an excellent presentation.

Steps for Network Marketing Presentation

1. **Introduction.**
2. **Company Profile**
3. **Products and services**
4. **Business opportunity**

First Step is Introduction –

It should include an overview of the network marketing industry. And a clear picture of the general network marketing or direct selling industry.

The second step is Company Profile –

This step includes information about the particular company.

- Complete profile.
- Date on which it legally came into existence.
- Its founder members, Managing Director, etc.
- It's Main Headquarter location & branches.
- Its product manufacturing industries.

The third step is the Company's Products –

This step includes presenting the products and services provided by the company and its benefits to people.

The fourth step is Business Plan –

Now we take our listeners to the business opportunity, which is our main step. As the purpose of showing the complete presentation is to make the listeners join the Network Marketing Company.

So we must,

Make a good base before we show the business plan.

Mr. Bhupendra Pal first explains the 4 categories of people on the basis of time and money, before he presents an actual business plan.

First category people,

People who have neither time nor money.
Second category people,
People who have a lot of time, but no money.
Third category people,
People who have no time, but they have money.
Forth category people,
People who have both time and money in balance.

He asks a question:- **"Which category you want to be?"**

99%, people say that they want to be in category four, which has both time and money in balance.

After their answer, he tells

"An opportunity that I am going to present in front of you has the potential to provide both time & financial freedom."

Then he starts the main presentation of the business opportunity.

Therefore, when we create a strong base before presenting the actual plan or opportunity, this becomes an effective presentation—also, the chances of prospect to associate conversion increase to the maximum.

As we know, 80% of problems in life are due to finances.

So, everyone wants an extra income. This can also become a switch (base) to lead our presentation to business opportunity with some more curiosity.

Maximum people don't know how to have a balance of time, money, and energy.

In childhood and teenage life –

We are full of energy and have a lot of time, but we don't have money,

In adult life –

We don't have time. But we have money and energy.

In old age –

We have money, but we are over with both time and energy.

So, if we want a balance of all the three-time, money and energy, we must join the network marketing business, which can provide us the balance of all three. So, this can also be a switch (base) from product presentation to business opportunity presentation.

Many network marketing distributors struggle in switching from product service to business opportunity. So they can use the above-discussed ways to have an effective presentation.

ppp

FIFTEEN
Follow-Up skills

"Showing hidden secrets of success in the network marketing to the prospects - is the right way of follow-up"

The presentation's main objective is that we want our prospect to convert to our client or associate.

But presentation has only a 5% contribution to the prospect building, whereas, the significant 95% contribution is through **'Follow up.'**

What is a follow-up?

In simple words through follow up, we give reasons to our prospects for following –

1. **'Why to become an associate' or**
2. **'Why to join our company, or**
3. **'Why to buy our products and services**

In the follow-up, we mainly strengthen the reasons for **'WHY.'**

We try to give strong reasons to prospects to join a network marketing company or direct selling company.

Let's understand, follow up with the help of the illustration.

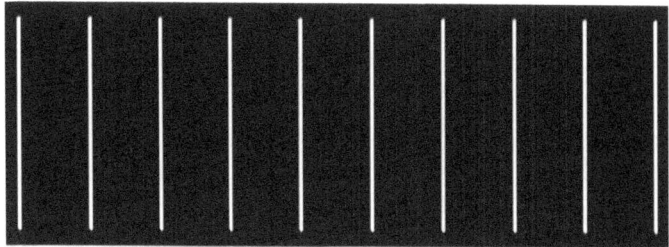

We can see ten lines, for prospects, these are simple vertical lines. But for a network marketer, these are not ten vertical lines but a hidden car in it.

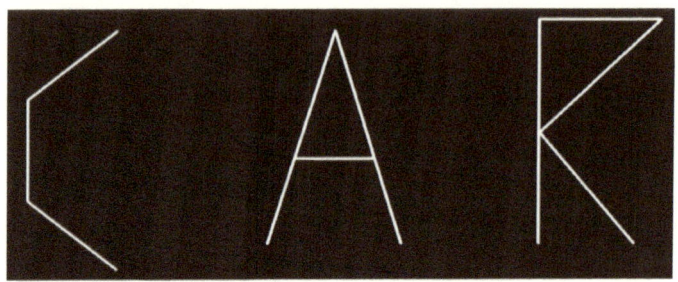

So, thisis the art of follow-up

Showing hidden secrets of success in the network marketing to the prospects is the right way of follow-up.

A strong vision and courage plays a vital role in network marketing follow up

When we show our plan, the maximum time people deny or reject. Therefore we need the courage to handle it.

And, again, try to follow up with them; showing them a strong vision that success is present in this opportunity.

Success may not be visible initially, but with time, it can be achieved with the right training and education.

We have an ample opportunity as there are more than 135 crore people in India. Keeping a strong vision of 135 crore people as prospects, we can achieve significant success, and then rejections failures won't affect much. It is also a strong follow point because people think that they don't know many people.

When we tell them that we have 135 crore of population who can be our prospects, this becomes a strong reason for them to join.

In the follow-up, we can tell people that the network marketing industry's education and training system is so strong that any ordinary person with zero skills can develop himself with all the essential skills of the 21st century.

Another point of follow-up is –

That there is little or no investment required joining the network marketing business.

So, even if anyone fails, then there is nothing much to lose.

When we do any traditional business, we have very few people to support us that include mostly our family, a few relatives and friends. But in the network marketing industry, there is an extensive support system that provides a strong system that is ready to help us support us in the form of our up-lines and other team members.

Thus, we will be able to realize the power of network marketing that can give success which a person can dream.

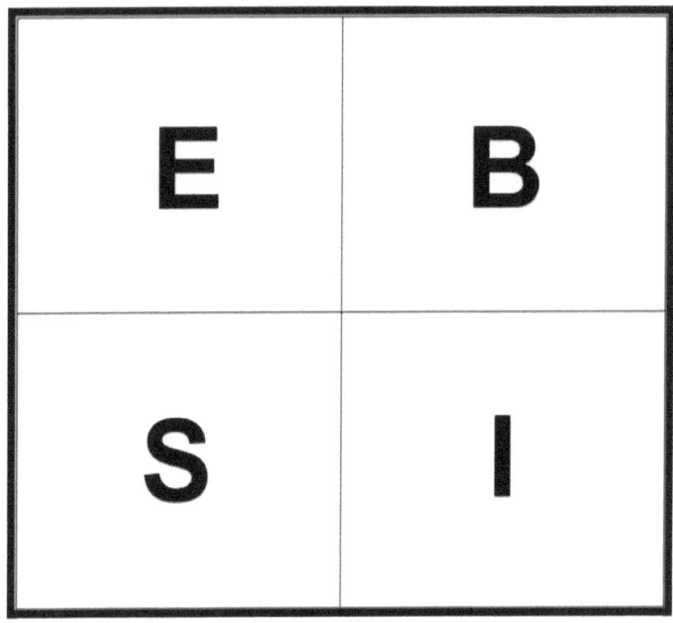

ESBI concept –

We all know about the ESBI concept,
E- Employee,
S- Small Business,
B- Business Owner, and
I - Investor

E (Employee) & S (Small Business) are the quadrants that show the Active Income Zone,

95% of people are in E and S quadrant.

B (Business) &I (Investor) belong to the Passive Income category,

Only 5% of people are in this quadrant.

95% hold only 5% of the total wealth, whereas 5% have almost 95% of the total wealth.

Let's understand this with an example.

There are two ponds.

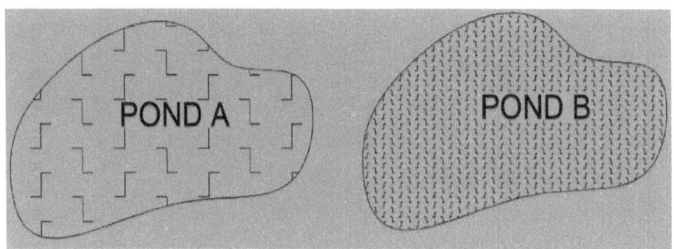

- **Pond A has 5 fishes**
- **Pond B has 95 fishes**.

Let's assume that you are a fisherman. Then, at which pond you will prefer to do fishing?

The answer is quite obvious; you will go for pond B.

People want to get fishes, but they are still sitting at pond A.

How will they become successful?

Therefore, we must switch our quadrant from the employ or self-employed zone to the business quadrant to attain more probability of success.

Another point of follow up –

It is the understanding of the power of network marketing.

People say, "This is just people joining or chain making business" and "We will have to urge people for all the time," etc. Similar feedbacks come when we talk about our network marketing business opportunity.

We must tell them about the three major powers.

Power of money

There are few families, like Ambanis, Adanis, Birla & Tata, which control almost 60-70% of the nation's economy.

Power of position

Bureaucrats, politicians, ministers, etc., who are in the government they have the control of position.

Power of Association

The Association of People is the most significant power to change the nation's Constitution.

So we must tell them the joining people is the power of Association. We can ask our friends that "can you work 100 hours in a day?" Friends will be surprised because we all have 24 hours a day. When we say, we do work for more than a hundred hours; an ordinary person will consider us a fool.

But as a network marketer, we know that not only a hundred, but a thousand ten thousand and even one lakh hours of work in a day is possible.

Let's understand this with an example.

If we hold a network of a hundred people, and every person is working for one hour in a day. Then, because of the Association, the total work done will be hundred hours a day.

We can work in multiple cities, states, or even countries, just sitting at one place. Lakhs and lakhs of hours, we can handle only by using one hour a day. So, this is the power of Network Marketing. This point can be a strong point of follow-up.

Visualization and skill of storytelling should be so strong that we can make our prospect visualize the dream life that can be achieved through this business.

Mr. Bhupendra Pal says,

"So many times when I used to spend lakhs and lakhs of money in experiencing luxurious holidays in various countries, at the same time, my account used to get credited with amount more than I spend."

Thus, this is a stress-free business that can be managed from any part of the world.

We shouldn't only connect ourselves to the luxury car or lifestyle of a successful network marketer, but we must learn the skills, habits, and values of that person, which led him to the massive success.

Mr. Bhupendra Pal says,

"Don't connect to my BMW but learn how I grow to BMW's level."

In network marketing in starting - we are an active source of income. We work, and we get money in the form of monthly payout or weekly payout.

But with time, when we develop a big business and create independent leaders in our team, this business starts giving passive income sources.

How to follow up with college-going students?

To college students, the benefits of Network Marketing can be explained through a comparison –

- College going students without direct selling

- College going students with direct selling

College going students (Without direct selling)

1. Only get Academic education.
2. Students waste their free time relaxing, playing games, self-entertainment etc.
3. Students depend on family for all financial and other needs.
4. After college, students may get an average 15,000 to 20,000 per month salary job.
5. After four to five years- The salary might increase to double the amount. For example, 15-20K per month salary might increase to 30-40K per month.
6. Growth is limited. For example, an assistant engineer can maximum becomes an executive engineer in the next 4 to 5 years.

College going students (with direct selling)

1. Get both academic education as we get the opportunity to learn life skills.
2. Students utilize the free time with meeting people who give motivation, as well as learning.
3. Direct selling gives a genuine opportunity to generate part-time income and become self-dependent.
4. After college, students can choose either job or direct selling business as a full-time business.

5. After four to five years in direct selling - If they worked with dedication, then monthly income can become three to four lakh to even ten to twelve lakh.
6. Growth is in our own hands. One who starts as a small distributor with zero income can grow to become a top distributor with high income.

So these were the few points through which follow up can be done.

ppp

SIXTEEN

Attributes of a Successful Networker

> *"Our Guru or Mentor in Network marketing is our active growing Up-line."*

Ten Main attributes

1. **Be crystal clear**
2. **Being Teachable**
3. **Accountability**
4. **Being opportunist**
5. **Visionary**
6. **Being Generous**
7. **Good Listener**
8. **Uplifting others**
9. **Always be a learner**
10. **Dreamer & doer**

First attribute - Be crystal clear

We need to be crystal clear of 'What we want in life?'

Many people join network marketing, but they don't know "Why exactly network marketing?"

They don't have any clarity of what they want to become in life.

Mr. Bhupendra Pal quotes his own life experience –

In college, when he got introduced to network marketing for the first time. He slowly understood all the aspects of network marketing and how this business can help him.

He compared this business to all the points that he had made for what he want in life.

He had a clear vision of what type of life he wanted to live. For this, he had made few points:-

· To become a successful person.
· Never to work under pressure.
· To work freely without any boss.
· Never to follow anybody's order & dominance.
· To live life on his own terms.
· To achieve time and financial freedom.

All these above points were in his mind since childhood. From, very young age, he had a clear vision in his mind.

The network marketing business seemed the only opportunity by which Mr. Bhupendra Pal could change the family's financial situation and it was according to the life he wanted to live. His mind was clear that the job will give him only a linear growth, but network marketing can make him achieve financial freedom.

Therefore a strong reason to join network marketing came to his mind.

A Complete clarity that –Network Marketing is the only business that can lead to success and allow him to live life on his own terms and conditions with full time and financial freedom.

Thus, the **'WHY- Factor'** became so strong in college itself, that while doing all classes, all assignments, he managed network marketing business very well.

He used to go for meetings, business trips, along with studies. He almost stopped the regular visits to his own home. He even started skipping the important festivals, like the Dussehra & Diwali.

In every holiday, he used to invest his time in developing his business. He had a clear vision in his mind that once his business is developed and his target of financial freedom is achieved then festivals could be celebrated almost every day.

His family tried to convince him to drop this business and concentrate only on studies because they wanted him to become a government officer.

One of his uncle asked him,

"How much do you earn?

Mr. Bhupendra Pal said, "5,000/- to 10,000/- per month."

It was a struggling phase when he was developing his business.

His uncle who was retired government service said,

"For just 5,000/- to 10,000/- you are working so hard, not coming to home, even in festivals, you keep running here and there. Taking so much tension for such a small amount?"

He again said pointing on himself - "See me; I am retired from a high post, so many privileges I am getting. Also, I made a big house."Then he added -

"You please stop wasting time and energy on business and try to focus more on becoming a government official like me."

This way, his uncle tried to pursue him.

Mr. Bhupendra Pal replied very politely -

"What all you said is right, uncle, but I am not working for 5,000 to 10,000, but I am working for complete financial freedom."

Therefore, the clarity of mind was so strong that even family, relatives all together couldn't convince him to drop his business.

Many people drop network marketing when they don't have a clear mindset & thus, they get convinced by family and other relatives or friends.

But when the question -

'Why am I working towards this goal?'

The answer to this is crystal clear, we can enjoy even in the struggling phase too. But unclear mindset only leads to confusion. People make mistakes by getting influenced by multiple people.

Mr. Bhupendra Pal says,

"Do take inspiration from all but follow your own thought process."

We get inspired by Virat Kohli, doesn't mean that we must take a bat and start playing cricket.

We get inspired by Shahrukh Khan, doesn't mean that we join the National School of Drama to become an actor.

Our thought process should be – to use the inspiration of their hard work, focus & dedication, in this network marketing business; and try to excel.

Mr. Bhupendra Pal says, -

"I had full clarity of 'Why Network Marketing?' I had strong reasons, so this clear mindset contributed a lot to my success."

But on the other hand, people fail as their mind is always fluctuating.

Therefore having clarity in mind is an attribute of a successful networker.

Second attribute - Being Teachable

Maximum people think that they know everything. They are not teachable. Up-line keeps telling them –

- To follow the system,
- Give time to self-development,
- Read books,
- Watch motivational videos etc.
- Make a list of prospects, and,
- Attend all the meetings

But some people don't take it seriously. As a result, they fail in network marketing. Thus, not being teachable leads to a downfall in network marketing.

To become successful, we need to follow the proper system provided by the company. If we are not teachable, not ready to follow and understand the system, taught by our up-line, we will surely proceed to failure.

Network Marketing is a business of duplication which must be followed as it is and the same to be taught to the down-line.

But many a time, few people become rigid, they keep cross-questioning against the system like

"Why should I make a list?" or

"Why should I attend meetings?

Mr. Bhupendra Pal says, -

"People, who keep on questioning & doubting the system, such people with ego & rigidity, never succeed."

He further says,

"I never questioned my up-line. They kept guiding me, and I kept converting their teachings into actions."

This attribute of being teachable is essential for becoming prosperous in any field.

Simplicity plays a major role in network marketing.

There are five main points that every network marketing company has in common in its education and training system. –

1. To use and recommend company products & services.
2. Improving personality & communication.
3. Joining every meeting
4. Teaching important skills - Invitation, Presentation, Follow up, and Objection handling.
5. Remain in regular contact with your active growing upline.

Mr. Bhupendra Pal says –

"To become successful in life, we need to become a good student first; for this, we must surrender to our teacher or guru."

Our Guru in network marketing is our active growing up-line. All top successful people like Sachin Tendulkar, Virat Kohli, Sharukh Khan, etc. have become successful because they are teachable.

They trained themselves and became experts in their fields because of their Guru. So, being teachable is an important attribute.

Third attribute - Accountability

Relations & mutual understandings are the foundation stone of network marketing. Relations develop with faith. Faith comes when we start taking responsibility for our words i.e., developing accountability.

People join network marketing because they believe in us, as on the very first day, they don't get a chance to see the company's headquarter or meet the company's Managing Director.

They join network marketing only because they have faith on us. Trust develops when our actions and words are both in synchronization. When our stories that we speak don't match with our efforts, then people start losing faith in us.

We must develop synchronization of words and actions. We must become accountable for our stories to build trust in other people.

Actions like,

· Always reaching on scheduled time.

· Giving more importance to other's time and efforts.

· Making promises and fulfilling them even in all situations.

These actions help in developing trust. Such a person is never alone, even in the difficult situations as his team strongly supports him.

Accountability creates faith and strengthens the relationship. The base of every business is faith which comes with responsibility; therefore it's an essential attribute of a successful networker.

Fourth attribute - Being opportunist

Being an opportunist means to make the best use of all opportunities or advantages.

Mr. Bhupendra Pal explains this attribute with his college life experience - College students used to study only during exam days whereas, in other days, they used to waste time in fun and entertainment. But unlike other students, Mr. Bhupendra Pal utilized this free time during college as an opportunity to do something, so that after college, he wouldn't face any tension for a job.

During three years of college, Mr. Bhupendra Pal developed his business so well that he had an excellent opportunity to join network marketing as soon as he passed college as a full-time business.

Maximum people take time very casually, and therefore time takes them casually. They miss all opportunities in life.

Many people in network marketing also start developing a casual behavior. They start taking their links and prospects for granted by reaching late or skipping meetings. As a result, new distributors start leaving them and slowly their business fails.

Therefore, Mr. Bhupendra Pal says,

"Every link in network marketing is a big opportunity; even a single new distributor can bring immense success to the business."

Thus, a successful network marketer has an attribute that he is always opportunist.

Fifth attribute – Visionary

Visionary means having a strong vision for the future.

A successful networker has a strong vision of:

- Where he is right now?
- Where he has to reach?
- What he has to achieve.

This clear vision of the next target must be always there in the mind of a network marketer.

Mr. Bhupendra Pal says,

"The biggest problem in India is unemployment. Network marketing is the only platform that can help many people, not only by providing opportunities to earn, but also to learn - 21st century's most important skills like personality development, communication skills, sales and marketing"

He has a strong vision that people at mass level needs network marketing.

So, being visionary is also an attribute of a successful network marketer.

Sixth attribute - Being generous

As our level of success increases, our learning attitude, our humbleness and gratitude must keep increasing.

'Otherwise, as success enters the brain, it causes downfall.'

Success should be directly proportional to humbleness.

When a person starts taking ownership of the worldly things, the arrogance increases.

It's essential to remain humble and thankful, especially for our family, who sacrificed a lot for our upbringing.

We can't deny the fact that so much struggle they did for us. Also, we can't deny the contribution of our teachers who taught us to become better.

In network marketing, too, there is a significant contribution of upline in training and developing us. So we should be thankful and remain humble.

Like, trees bend when food grows on it. Similarly, more humbleness must come with more success.

Seventh attribute - Becoming a good listener

Listening is essential for every communication, but it's a problem because most of us listen only to reply, not to understand the other person.

A successful network marketer always listens to understand the needs and requirements of the prospect or the down-line. He properly listens to every word, understands it, and then gives the most suitable solution.

Many leaders in Network Marketing don't listen. They think they are above all, so they don't need to listen to anyone. Such people are full of arrogance. The down-line of such people doesn't oppose them in front of them, but slowly and steadily, they start getting away from them. Thus, it affects our business. We must remember that listening is essential to understand another person. So, we should be a good listener first.

Therefore allowing others to speak first and listening to them & understanding them is also an essential attribute of a successful networker.

Eighth attribute –

Genuine interest in uplifting other people.

It is essential. Mr. Bhupendra Pal says –

"In this business, we should think of other people's success more than our personal success."

In network marketing, other's success or upliftment results in our own upliftment. We grow as our network grows. So we must plan for the success of others.

In network marketing, we use business to build other people. We don't use people to build a business, like it happens in other businesses.

So we must give the right motivation, right thinking, and proper mindset to other people.

And therefore, uplifting them with genuine interest is an essential attribute of a successful networker.

Ninth attribute - Always be a learner.

We should work on our-self continuously. There should be a strong willingness to learn more and more.

The person who thinks that he has learned everything now and doesn't need to know more is making a big mistake.

A successful network marketer has a habit of learning new things every day. He tries to imbibe good qualities and skills, even from their juniors or down-lines.

The mistake that maximum people do in network marketing is to change other people, but don't change themselves.

When we concentrate on our learning and

Self-development, our team will also develop because it reflects the leader. So, if a leader is lazy and has a habit of procrastination, the team will also develop the same practice. But if a leader is enthusiastic and is consistently upgrading himself with new skills, the team will also follow him and create the same habit and improve their productivity.

So, the main attribute of a successful networker is that he remains a learner.

Tenth attribute - dreamer and doer

Today we find maximum people are dreamers. When we ask them,

"What you want in life?"

They will reply with,

"I want BMW, Audi, Mercedes, big Villa and a luxurious life etc."

When we ask them,

"What is your plan?" "How will you achieve them?"

Then maximum, people are blank, they dream for BMW Lamborghini and big, expensive luxury cars, but their actions do not even deserve a Maruti 800.

So to become successful, one of the essential habits is that we must not limit to be a dreamer only but we must become an action taker. We need to work on our dreams.

The Dream must be followed by proper planning and preparation to make it a reality. The next step should be proper execution, as per the plan.

With full discipline, focus, and dedication, a person can become successful.

Mr. Bhupendra Pal says,

> ***"I saw a dream and achieved it because I don't only dream, but I have proper planning to achieve it."***

It is an excellent attribute of a successful person that all the following five questions must be clear as per the dream.

- 'Who?
- 'Where?'
- 'Why?'
- 'When?'
- 'What?'

We have a lot of expectations from life. But do we have expectations from our own-self?

We need to introspect and ask our self –

- 'Are we making a proper plan?' Or
- 'Are we working, according to the list?' Or
- 'Our actions worth, can they lead us to success?'

Successful people have more expectations from themselves than life.

Mr. Bhupendra Pal says,

> ***"I always try to live up to the expectations of what I have for myself."***

Therefore to become successful, we need to develop this attribute of becoming a 'doer'.

When we imbibe all the attributes discussed in the above paragraphs and pages, we start achieving network marketing success.

SEVENTEEN
CONCLUSION

This is a business of

"GIVING"

To sum up, I would like to thank Mr. Bhupendra Pal for sparing time to complete this book.

The tips and strategies given in this book are all practical, as they are performed by sir himself with tremendous results. So, this book can prove to be a helpful guideline for every network marketer, who is willing to attain success.

Soon, we will be coming up with more practical knowledge, including tips and strategies by -

Mr. Bhupendra Pal himself on- **How to become a 7-figure earner in Network Marketing**.

(Upcoming Book -)

'Average Earner'

To

'Multiple 7-figure earner'

(Tips & strategies by Mr. Bhupendra Pal)

Follow

Mr. Bhupendra Pal

Website: -

https://www.bhupendrapal.com/

ᗞᗞᗞ

Instagram ID: -

https://instagram.com/bhupendra4u?igshid=1dptf7u2el69c

ᗞᗞᗞ

About The Author

Supreet Batra, author of 'Slow Start to Super Success' is an architect, designer, and a motivational writer. His writing style makes perfect sense and is based on his phenomena that an ordinary person with determination and dedication can raise to the heights of success. There is a focus on some cutting edge stuff in his books, which one requires for a highly successful business. Love and enthusiasm for writing is boundless in his books.

▷▷▷

www.ingramcontent.com/pod-product-compliance
Lightning Source LLC
Chambersburg PA
CBHW030813180526
45163CB00003B/1267